Bella and the Kite

An English/French Book

Bella et le Cerf-volant

Une histoire bilingue anglais-français

Chris Jacob

Bella and the Kite, Bella et le Cerf-volant
An English/French Book/ Une histoire bilingue anglais-français

Images by Christabelle, www.christabelle.co.uk

French translation by Audrey Langlassé
http://www.alacarte-translations.com/

Published by www.20wordsaweek.com and CreateSpace

ISBN-13: 978-1546592495

ISBN-10: 1546592490

Acknowledgements

To a little girl, a windy day and a kite

Remerciements

À une petite fille et un cerf-volant, un jour de grand vent

An important note on the use of the Passé Simple

This book is aimed at more advanced early learners, and so the passé simple has been used in preference to the passé composé in combination with the imparfait, another past tense.

We provide this note to assist any learners who may be unfamiliar with the use of the passé simple.

The passé simple is the literary equivalent of the passé composé, used predominantly in narratives and formal writing.

We have highlighted each use of the passé simple and placed the infinitive form of the verb on the French translation page.

This page is intentionally left blank.

Bella looked out the window and thought today was the perfect day.

It was not too hot, it was not too cold, it was not foggy, it was not snowing, it was not humid it was not raining.... not even a drizzle... It was a lovely windy day. Perfect for flying her new kite....

Bella **regarda** par la **fenêtre** et se dit qu'il faisait **aujourd'hui** un temps idéal.

Il ne **faisait** ni trop **chaud**, ni trop **froid** ; il n'y avait ni **brume**, ni **neige**, ni **orage**, ni **pluie**... pas même une petite **bruine**. C'était une belle journée **venteuse**. Le temps idéal pour **faire voler** son nouveau **cerf-volant**...

Key words/Mots clés

- Regarder = to look at
- La fenêtre = window
- Aujourd'hui = today
- Faire chaud = to be hot
- Faire froid = to be cold
- La brume = fog
- La neige = snow
- L'orage = storm
- La pluie = rain
- La bruine = drizzle
- Venteux = windy
- Faire voler un cerf-volant = to fly a kite

After all the necessary preparations were made, and her dad had assembled the kite, Bella marched out into her back garden. Bella had previously calculated that the garden was just big enough to fly a kite in.

Bella took up her prime flying position on top of a small mound of earth.

Bella's mum called from the house, "isn't it a bit too windy for flying a kite?"

Bella called back, "there is no such thing as too windy" (she was a very brave little girl).

Une fois tous les **préparatifs** terminés et le cerf-volant assemblé par son papa, Bella **sortit** d'un pas décidé dans son jardin. **Selon** ses calculs, le jardin était juste assez grand pour faire voler un cerf-volant.

Bella **se mit** en position de **lancement** sur un petit **monticule de terre**.

De **la maison**, sa maman lui **cria** : — Est-ce qu'il n'y a pas un peu trop de **vent** pour sortir un cerf-volant ?

— Il n'y a jamais trop de vent ! Bella lui **répondit**. (C'était une petite fille très **courageuse.**)

Key words/Mots clés

- Les préparatifs = preparations
- Sortir d'un pas décidé = to march out
- Selon = according to
- Se mettre en position = to take up a position
- En position de lancement = launching position
- Le monticule de terre = mound of earth
- La maison = house
- Le vent = wind
- Crier = to call out
- Répondre = to answer
- Courageux = brave

Bella took hold of the kite's string line and directed her Dad into position.

He took the kite and readied himself, holding the kite aloft ready for Bella's release signal.

"Are you sure this kite is meant for children?" he shouted over the noise of the wind.

Elle **s'empara** de la ligne du cerf-volant et **donna** des instructions à son papa.

Celui-ci **prit** le cerf-volant et **le tint en l'air**, prêt à le **lâcher** au signal de Bella.

— Tu es bien sûre que ce cerf-volant est pour les enfants ? **cria**-t-il pour couvrir **le bruit** du vent.

Key words/Mots clés

- S'emparer = to take hold of
- Donner = to give
- Prendre = to take
- Tenir = to hold
- En l'air = aloft
- Lâcher = to release
- Crier = to shout
- Le bruit = noise

"Of course it is Daddy, you worry too much," replied Bella raising her voice as loud as possible.

"It is just that it looks quite big," bellowed Bella's Dad as the wind nearly blew him over.

Bella could not hear what he said, she was focusing on the perfect moment to release the kite…then it came….she knew it was time…

"Release the kite Daddy… quick," she hollered.

— Évidemment, Papa, tu t'**inquiètes** trop, **répliqua** Bella du plus **fort** qu'elle **pût**.

— C'est juste qu'il a l'air **vraiment** grand, **hurla**-t-il alors que le vent **faillit** le **renverser**.

Bella ne l'**entendit** pas ; très **concentrée**, elle **attendait** le moment idéal pour lâcher le cerf-volant... Il **finit** par arriver... Elle **sut** alors que c'était le bon moment...

— Lâche le cerf-volant Papa, vite ! **cria**-t-elle.

Key words/Mots clés

- S'inquiéter = to worry
- Répliquer = to reply
- Fort = loud
- Pouvoir = can
- Vraiment = quite
- Hurler = to bellow
- Faillir = nearly do something
- Renverser = to blow over
- Entendre = to hear
- Concentré = focused
- Attendre = to wait for
- Finir par = to end up
- Savoir = to know
- Crier = to holler

Up the kite zoomed until the line was taut. Bella's Dad craned his neck as the kite continued to rise higher and higher.

"That's funny," he thought to himself. "Should the kite be going as high as that?"

He looked down, and to his horror and amazement, he saw little Bella was being hoisted up into the sky.

Le cerf-volant **monta en flèche** jusqu'à ce que la ligne soit **tendue**. Son père **se tordit** le **cou** pour le **suivre des yeux** alors qu'il continuait son **ascension**.

« C'est drôle, se dit-il. Est-ce normal qu'il **monte** si **haut** ? »

Son regard **suivit** la ligne, et horreur, il **découvrit** que sa fille était **soulevée** dans les airs.

Key words/Mots clés

- Monter en flèche = to zoom up
- Tendu = taut
- Se tordre le cou = to crane one's neck
- Suivre des yeux/du regard = to follow with one's eyes
- L'ascension = ascent
- Monter = to go up
- Haut = high
- Découvrir = to discover
- Soulever = to hoist

Bella's Dad ran as quick as he could towards her. He lunged through the air and tried to grasp hold of her shoe. Bella however had not quite perfected the art of tying her shoe laces and unfortunately it slipped off of her foot. Her Daddy fell forward flat onto his face still clutching the shoe.

Bella let out a shriek but, being sensible, she held on as tight as she could to the kite's line and she soared into the sky.

Il **se mit** à **courir** le plus vite possible vers elle, puis **bondit** pour **tenter** de l'**attraper** par la **chaussure**. **Malheureusement**, Bella n'**ayant** pas encore parfaitement **maîtrisé** l'art des **lacets**, la chaussure **glissa** de son pied. Son père **s'étala** de tout son long serrant dans sa main **le soulier**.

La petite fille **laissa échapper** un **cri**, mais, pleine de bon sens, elle **pensa** à **s'agripper** de toutes ses forces à la ligne du cerf-volant lorsqu'elle **s'envola** dans **le ciel**.

Key words/Mots clés

- Se mettre à = to start doing
- Courir = to run
- Bondir = to jump
- Tenter de = to try to
- Attraper = to grasp
- La chaussure = shoe
- Malheureusement = unfortunately
- Ayant = having
- Maîtriser = to master
- Les lacets = laces
- Glisser = to slip off
- S'étaler = to fall flat
- Le soulier = shoe
- Laisser échapper = to let out
- Le cri = shriek
- Penser à = to think of
- S'aggripper = to hold on tight
- S'envoler = to soar
- Le ciel = sky

The wind whisked her and the kite up and away and in the direction of the neighbour's house.

Mr Jones, the man who lived next door, was a grumpy sort and he was out in his back garden trying to put a cover over his beloved sports car. He was not doing very well as the wind kept blowing the cover off. As a result, he was even more grumpy than usual.

"Blast this cover," he said to himself for the fifteenth time of trying to attach it to the car. The cover had managed to wrap itself right around him and it looked like he was wearing a large and peculiar dress.

Le vent **l'emportait** avec le cerf-volant, **toujours** plus haut en direction de **la maison d'à côté**.

Elle était habitée par M. Jones, un homme **grincheux**, qui était sorti dans son jardin pour **tenter** de mettre une **bâche** sur sa voiture de sport adorée. Les choses ne se passaient pas très bien, car le vent ne **cessait** de **repousser** la bâche. Il était donc de plus **mauvaise humeur** que d'habitude.

« **Maudite** bâche », se **dit**-il en essayant de la fixer à sa voiture pour la **quinzième** fois. La bâche avait fini par s'**enrouler** autour de lui et il **avait l'air** de porter une grande robe un peu bizarre.

Key words/Mots clés

- Emporter = to whisk away
- Toujours = always
- La maison d'à côté = the house next door
- Grincheux = grumpy
- La bâche = cover
- Ne cesser de faire = to keep doing
- Repousser = to blow off
- La mauvaise humeur = bad mood
- Maudit = blasted
- Se dire = to say to oneself
- Quinzième = fifteenth
- S'enrouler = to wrap around
- Avoir l'air = to look like

When Bella's family had first moved in next door to Mr Jones, Bella had been playing with water balloons. She had accidently (although slightly on purpose) thrown a water balloon over the fence that had landed exactly on top of Mr Jones' head.

For some reason, after that incident, Bella and Mr Jones were not the best of friends.

À l'époque où la famille de Bella avait **emménagé** à côté de chez M. Jones, Bella jouait beaucoup avec des **bombes à eau**. Elle en avait, accidentellement (mais un peu **exprès** aussi), lancé une, de l'autre côté de la **barrière**, qui avait **atterri pile** sur la tête de son **voisin**.

Curieusement, depuis cet incident, Bella et M. Jones n'étaient pas très bons amis.

Key words/Mots clés

- Emménager = to move in
- La bombe à eau = water balloon
- Exprès = on purpose
- La barrière = fence
- Atterrir = to land
- Pile = right on
- Le voisin = neighbour
- Curieusement = strangely enough

Bella looked down from her precarious position; she was dangling like a bauble on a Christmas tree.

"Help," she shouted. "I am up here," she screamed at the top of her lungs flailing her legs around hoping to catch Mr Jones' attention.

Mr Jones was a bit hard of hearing and, given he was trapped by his car cover, he was a bit distracted.

En équilibre précaire, Bella **regarda** en bas ; elle se **balançait** comme une boule dans un arbre de Noël.

— Au secours, **hurla**-t-elle ! Je suis là-haut, **s'époumona**-t-elle en **agitant** les jambes dans **l'espoir** d'**attirer** l'attention de son voisin.

En plus d'être un peu **dur d'oreille**, M. Jones n'était pas très **concentré**, **empêtré** qu'il était dans sa bâche.

Key words/Mots clés

- L'équilibre = balance
- Se balancer = to dangle
- Hurler = to shout
- S'époumoner = to shout at the top of one's lungs
- Agiter = to flail
- L'espoir = hope
- Attirer = to attract
- Dur d'oreille = hard of hearing
- Concentré = focused
- Empêtré = trapped

Bella summoned up all her breath and shouted as loud as she could, "MR JONES!!!!" She frantically kicked her legs trying her best to catch his attention.

Mr Jones looked up to see the stupendous sight of little Bella flying over his garden. His jaw fell open as he witnessed Bella's remaining shoe come flying off her flailing foot.

He watched in amazement as Bella's shoe, like a guided missile, zoomed past just inches in front of his face. The flying shoe thwacked with a mighty force into the side of Mr Jones' precious sports car.... For a small shoe, it left a surprisingly big dent!

Bella **prit** une **profonde inspiration** et **vociféra** de toutes ses forces « M. JONES ! » en **bougeant** les jambes **dans tous les sens** pour **attirer** son attention.

M. Jones **leva les yeux**, et à sa plus grande **stupeur**, **vit** la petite Bella **survoler** son jardin.

Bouche bée, il **regarda** la **deuxième** chaussure de la fillette **se détacher** de son pied qui battait l'air et lui **frôler** le visage à **vive allure**, tel un missile téléguidé. La chaussure volante **vint s'écraser** brutalement sur **l'aile** de sa précieuse voiture de sport... Pour une petite chaussure, elle **laissa** une **sacrée** grosse **bosse** !

Key words/Mots clés

- Prendre = to take
- Profond = deep
- Inspiration = breath in
- Vociférer = to shout loudly
- Bouger = to move
- Dans tous les sens = in all directions
- Attirer = to catch
- Lever les yeux = to look up
- La stupeur = amazement
- Voir = to see
- Survoler = to fly over
- Être bouche bée = to be flabbergasted
- Regarder = to look at
- Deuxième = second
- Se détacher = to come off
- Frôler = to skim past
- À vive allure = at full speed
- Venir = to come
- S'écraser = to twack
- L'aile = wing
- Laisser = to leaver
- Sacré = quite
- La bosse = dent

Mr Jones, after he gathered his senses, started hopping up and down like an enraged rabbit. Unfortunately, as he was still ensnared by the cover, he quickly lost his footing.

Mrs Jones had been in the kitchen reading a magazine. Noticing the commotion, she looked out of the window just in time to observe her husband do an impressive pirouette before falling, making a large splash, into their pond.

Mrs Jones immediately sprung up from her seat and dashed out to the pond as fast as her legs would carry her. She was desperately worried. She had bought a new gold fish the week before and was terrified it might have been injured by Mr Jones.

Une fois **revenu** de sa surprise, M. Jones **commença** à **sauter dans tous les sens** comme un lapin enragé. **Malheureusement**, comme il était encore **coincé** dans la bâche, il **perdit** rapidement l'équilibre.

Mme Jones, **de son côté**, **lisait** un magazine dans sa cuisine. **Alertée** par **le bruit**, elle **regarda** par la fenêtre juste à temps pour voir son mari faire une **impressionnante** pirouette et tomber dans leur **bassin** avec un gros plouf.

Elle **bondit** immédiatement de son siège et courut vers le bassin **à toute vitesse**. Elle était **extrêmement inquiète**. Elle avait acheté la semaine **précédente** un nouveau poisson rouge et **tremblait à l'idée** que M. Jones l'ait **blessé** dans sa **chute**.

Key words/Mots clés

- Revenir = to recover
- Commencer = to start
- Sauter = to jump
- Dans tous les sens = up and down
- Malheureusement = unfortunately
- Coincé = ensnared
- Perdre = to lose
- De son côté = as for
- Lire = to read
- Alerté = aware of
- Le bruit = noise
- Regarder = to look
- Impressionnant = impressive
- Le bassin = pond
- Bondir = to jump
- À toute vitesse = as quick as possible
- Extrêmement = extremely
- Inquiet = worried
- Précédent = previous
- Trembler à l'idée = to be terrified just thinking that
- Blesser = to injure
- La chute = fall

Bella, despite her precarious predicament, chuckled at the sight of Mr Jones flopping about in the pond like a flabbergasted frog.

Mrs Jones had, in a bungled attempt at rescuing her beloved goldfish, decisively, but unfortunately for Mr Jones, inaccurately, swished a net over his head!

Malgré sa situation précaire, Bella ne **put s'empêcher** de rire en voyant M. Jones **affalé** dans le bassin **telle** une grenouille **médusée**.

Les efforts de Mme Jones pour sauver son poisson rouge adoré **tournèrent** très vite **au fiasco**. D'un geste décidé, mais **maladroit**, pour le plus grand **malheur** de M. Jones, elle **abattit** son **épuisette** sur la tête de son mari !

Key words/Mots clés

- Malgré = despite
- Pouvoir = can
- S'empêcher de = to refrain
- Rire = to chuckle
- Affalé = flopping
- Tel = like
- Médusé = flabbergasted
- Tourner au fiasco = to end in a fiasco
- Maladroit = awkward
- Le malheur = misfortune
- Abattre = to swish over
- L'épuisette = net

Although she was enjoying the spectacle, Bella's arms were really starting to ache.

Suddenly, a strong gust of wind blew and it propelled Bella higher, it scooped her up and away. Ignoring her aching arms, Bella gripped onto the kite's line as tightly as she could.

Bella was swept up high into the sky, and kept going up and up and up, so high that she started to shiver – the homes far below her looked like tiny match box houses.

Bien qu'amusée par ce spectacle, Bella commençait à **avoir** très **mal aux bras**.

Soudain, une forte **rafale souffla** ; elle **propulsa** la petite fille toujours plus haut dans les airs, l'emportant encore plus **loin**. **Oubliant** ses bras **endoloris**, elle **se cramponna** à la ligne du cerf-volant **de toutes ses forces**.

Balayée par le vent, elle ne cessait de **monter** dans le ciel, si haut qu'elle **commença** à **frissonner** : tout en bas, les maisons **ressemblaient** à de minuscules **boîtes d'allumettes**.

Key words/Mots clés

- Bien que = although
- Avoir mal aux bras = to have aching arms
- Le bras = arm
- La rafale = gust of wind
- Souffler = to blow
- Propulser = to propel
- Loin = far away
- Oublier = to ignore
- Endolori = aching
- Se cramponner = to grip
- De toutes ses forces = as tightly as possible
- Balayer = to sweep up
- Monter = to go up
- Commencer = to start
- Frissonner = to shiver
- Ressembler à = to look like
- La boîte d'allumettes = match box

As Bella went higher, curious birds began circling her.

One bold and large bird, a sea gull, started to circle very close to Bella's kite, getting closer and closer with every turn.

All of a sudden, like a diver bomber, it plummeted towards the kite. With one almighty flap of its large wings, it sent the kite into a spin, sending it, and Bella, tumbling earthwards.

Tandis que Bella montait, d'**étranges** oiseaux se **mirent** à l'**encercler**.

Une grande **mouette** en particulier, **intrépide**, **commença** à tourner très près **autour** du cerf-volant, s'en **rapprochant** à **chaque** tour.

Tout à coup, tel un **bombardier**, elle **plongea**. D'un battement **puissant** de ses grandes **ailes,** elle **envoya tourbillonner** le cerf-volant et Bella dans une **chute vertigineuse**.

Key words/Mots clés

- Tandis que = while
- Étrange = curious
- Se mettre à = to start
- Encercler = to circle
- La mouette = sea gull
- Intrépide = bold
- Commencer = to start
- Autour de = around
- Se rapprocher = to get closer
- Chaque = each
- Tout à coup = all of a sudden
- Le bombardier = diver bomber
- Plonger = to plummet
- Puissant = almighty
- L'aile = wing
- Envoyer = to send
- Tourbillonner = to spin
- La chute vertigineuse = breathtaking fall

Bella's started to panic...As her velocity increased however, and the earth hurtled towards her, she came to her senses...

She summoned all her remaining strength and yanked the line downwards, as if she were reining in a wild horse. Miraculously, the kite unfurled, bringing Bella's decent to a sudden end.

La panique **gagna** Bella... Cependant, **à mesure que** sa vitesse **augmentait** et que le sol se rapprochait **à vive allure,** elle **reprit ses esprits**.

Elle **rassembla** toute la force qui lui restait et **tira d'un coup sec** sur la ligne comme si elle **tentait** de **maîtriser** un cheval **sauvage**. Miracle ! Le cerf-volant **se déploya** et mit fin **brusquement** à la **descente** de Bella.

Key words/Mots clés

- Gagner = to gain
- À mesure que = as
- Augmenter = to increase
- À vive allure = at full speed
- Reprendre = to regain
- Les esprits = senses
- Rassembler = to gather
- Tirer d'un coup sec = to yank
- Tenter de = to attempt to
- Maîtriser = to rein in
- Sauvage = wild
- Se déployer = to unfurl
- Brusquement = suddenly
- La descente = descent

Bella looked below, and to her surprise and delight, she could see her family waving their arms frantically.

She again yanked the line of the kite, causing her to drop. Fortunately for Bella, she crash-landed directly into her Daddy, which meant that she tumbled onto the ground without a single scratch.

La petite fille **regarda** en bas, et quelles ne **furent** pas sa surprise et sa **joie** de voir sa famille lui **faire de grands gestes** !

Elle tira encore d'un coup sec sur la ligne du cerf-volant, ce qui la **fit** tomber. Heureusement, elle s'**écrasa** directement sur son père ; son **atterrissage** forcé se **fit ainsi sans la moindre égratignure**.

Key words/Mots clés

- Regarder = to look at
- Être = to be
- La joie = joy
- Faire de grands gestes = to wave frantically
- Faire = to make
- S'écraser = to crash-land
- L'atterrissage = landing
- Ainsi = therefore
- Sans = without
- Le moindre = the slightest
- L'égratignure = scratch

The impact of the crash made Bella lose her grip on the kite line. The wind suddenly picked up again, heaving the kite back up into the sky.

She sat on the ground by the side of her Daddy and watched it go soaring up higher and higher, until it was only just a speck.

Once the kite was barely visible, Bella turned to her Daddy and asked sweetly, “Can we get another kite?”

THE END

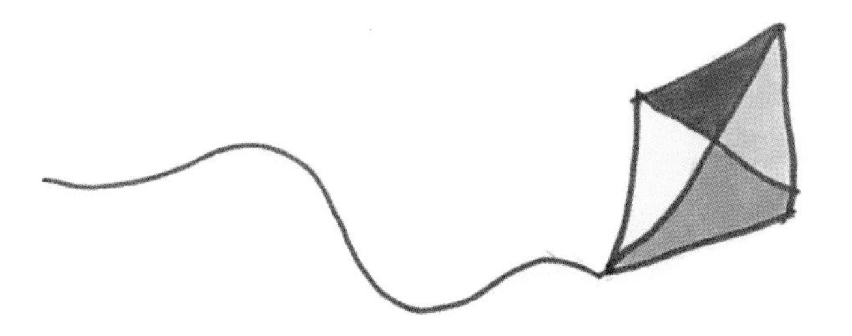

Sous l'impact, la fillette **lâcha** la ligne. Le vent **reprit** soudain **de la vigueur**, soulevant à nouveau le cerf-volant dans le ciel.

Assise par terre près de son père, Bella **suivit** des yeux son ascension **jusqu'à** ce qu'il ne soit plus qu'un **tout** petit **point**.

Lorsque le cerf-volant **eut** presque **disparu**, elle **se tourna** vers lui et lui **demanda** d'une voix douce : « Papa, est-ce qu'on peut en acheter un autre ? »

FIN

Key words/Mots clés

- Sous l'impact = under the impact
- Lâcher = to let out
- Reprendre de la vigueur = to pick up again
- Assis = sitting
- Suivre = to follow
- Jusqu'à = until
- Tout = only
- Le point = speck
- Lorsque = once
- Disparaître = to disappear
- Se tourner = to turn
- Demander = to ask

For suggestions and feedback please email us at **info@20wordsaweek.com** or visit **www.20wordsaweek.com**

We value your feedback....

Printed in Great Britain
by Amazon

78232210R00025